The Unlikely Achieveher: 11 Steps To A Happy & Prosperous Life

Lakisha L. Simmons, Ph.D.

ISBN-13: 978-0-578-41352-5

BRAVE CONSULTING LLC

Dedication

This book is dedicated to the family, friends, and teachers who have supported and encouraged me to be the AchieveHer I am today.

Table Of Contents

Introduction 1

Poise

1 Self-Awareness Assessment.. 9
2 Increase Your Self-Esteem 21
3 Define Your Passion & Purpose 27
4 Using Body Language 37

Persistence

5 Overcome Obstacles And Be Happy 53
6 Conflict Resolution... 59
7 Mental Health & Self Care.. 67

Prosperity

8 Achieve Your Goals.. 79
9 Education Changes Everything 87
10 Wealth Building 95
11 Achieve A Successful Career 107
Final Words Of Encouragement 115
About The Author...119

Introduction

"Don't let your past predict your future. Overcome those challenges and be poised, persistent and prosperous." — Lakisha L. Simmons, Ph.D.

Dear AchieveHer,

As a little girl growing up in Indiana, I had one wish. Each night I would pray that one day I would be happy. Not to be a millionaire, nor to be famous, but happy. I'm thankful that today, as an adult, I am happy.

My teen parents were high school sweethearts who married upon my conception. My father joined the Marines after high school graduation to make a better life for us. My mother didn't finish high school, but later in life achieved her GED. The distance between them became too much, their relationship became strained, and their marriage ended after a few short years. There were a lot of disagreements and hurt feelings between them that I will never understand. But their strained relationship left me in the middle and torn about whose side to take. As I became a preteen I witnessed things that no child should. I bounced around and lived with various family members as my mother was away figuring out her life. My father was living his own life as well. For some reason, I didn't fit into either of their lives. I was emotionally abandoned. But I'm thankful to the community of family members and friends that loved me and supported me through my childhood and adolescent years. I wouldn't be happy today if it weren't for those who went out of their way to care for me, let me live with them, and provided for my necessities while I attended high school and college.

Today, I have a positive relationship with my mother and my father. That wasn't the case when I was a child. But what I've learned through enduring family trauma (and drama) is that I am in control of the emotion of my relationships. With my actions, I can change the opinions, stances, and actions of others. In those cases where "it's just not working," I've learned to lovingly release myself from the situation.

Professionally, I am fulfilled in every way. As a professor, I have the honor of being a teacher, mentor and trusted advisor to hundreds of future business leaders each week. Teaching information systems, programming languages, and data science keeps me at the forefront of the world's most enabling technologies. As a scholar, I cure my intellectual curiosity by researching ways to improve teaching and learning and business processes by using cutting edge technologies. From that research, I learned there is a need to instill organization and time management skills in students early in the education process to develop successful students. I developed Homework Suite, a student planner and reminder app that allows students to bulk load their syllabus assignments one time and receive reminders during the semester. No more "I forgot".

Service wise, I'm fulfilled by mentoring and counseling young women in the life skills and soft skills training they need to be poised, persistent and prosperous in this world. I don't say all of that to brag about me, I say it to inspire you. I am just like you. You are just like me. And in this book, I share with you the characteristics that have helped me to live a happy life.

So, what does happiness look like to you? Think about these questions: If a genie magically appeared, what would you wish for? What would you do if you weren't afraid? If money was no concern, how would you spend your time?

Now briefly write how you visualize your happy life (find more life planning worksheets at www.theachieveHer.com):

My happy life is being at peace
retired
going to school
having good relationships & spending time with loved ones
having God in my life
living a healthy lifestyle

So, what does it mean to be an AchieveHer?

She is the epitome of a queen. She is highly successful and an influencer. She is strong, determined and always working to overcome obstacles. She is intelligent and wise due to her love for education. She has grace, dignity, confidence and high self-esteem. Ultimately, she possesses poise, persistence, and prosperity.

Are you ready to be an AchieveHer? You're ready to be an AchieveHer if...

You are ready to take a deep look at yourself and improve while owning who you are. You are ready to stop dealing with drama, lack of motivation, rejection, and/or unhappiness. You want to overcome any obstacle, achieve every goal and attract only good things to your life. You want to be prosperous and happy in your personal and professional life.

Get ready to learn all this and more. This workbook is organized into three parts: Poise, Persistence, and Prosperity. Poise is the graceful and elegant bearing in a person and in this part, you will work on discovering and owning who you are and transforming into a more poised woman. Persistence is persevering continuously, and in this part you will unlock the tiger in you and become more self-motivated and driven. Prosperity, characterized by success, luxury, opulence, or wealth, is having a good life (whatever that means to you). In the last section of the book you will learn the life skills you need to have the prosperous life you desire. Get ready to have a successful career, reach your financial goals, and not only live debt free, but also build wealth.

Book layout

Each chapter begins with a mantra or phrase used to enter meditation and bring intention into your life (Deepak Chopra, chopra.com). Read the mantra aloud and then close your eyes, take a deep breath, and repeat the mantra to yourself three times.

Next, do the challenge exercise. This will be a short exercise to engage you with the topic and open your mind and heart.

An inspirational quote and learning objectives follow. These two items help guide your work throughout the chapter. The chapter is full of open-ended questions and worksheet activities. There is also space for you to map out a new habit based on what you've learned. The last section is a space for reflection. Get out your highlighter, pen and paper and get ready to reach your full potential.

This is part of your personal development in becoming a success. I pray this guidebook leads you to discover who you are and helps you become who you aim to be. An *AchieveHer*. The most successful people make commitments and keep them, so let's get started with a commitment plan.

Commitment plan

To complete this guidebook, you must put a plan in place. Focus on completing this entire guidebook by a specific date. Set a realistic but aggressive goal. For example, one month, working through the book each night.

Commitment Plan

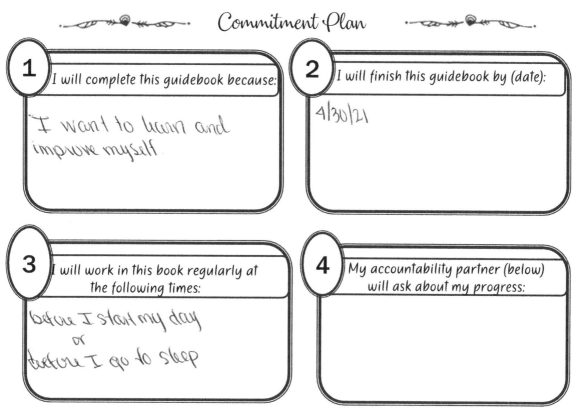

1 — I will complete this guidebook because:

I want to learn and improve myself.

2 — I will finish this guidebook by (date):

4/30/21

3 — I will work in this book regularly at the following times:

before I start my day
or
before I go to sleep

4 — My accountability partner (below) will ask about my progress:

I will reach my full potential and accomplish all my goals. I am an AchieveHer.

Poise

1 Self-awareness Assessment

Mantra

I love who I am, and I always strive to be a better person.

Challenge

Ask your best friend how you can be a better friend to her or him.

Quote:

> *"Start accepting people for who they are. The sooner you do this, the happier you will be because you will no longer expect them to be perfect."* — *Dr. Kisha Simmons*

Objectives are to become self-aware by:

1. Answering and analyzing a personality assessment

2. Determining how you can better communicate with others

3. Ceasing toxic behavior that keeps you from engaging in healthy relationships

This chapter is about maturing and becoming a better communicator, team player, friend, and confidante. It's not about changing who you are or your looks. To live a happy and successful life, you must first know yourself and what makes you happy. It's not easy to inspect your behavior, habits and communication style and identify where you must improve. It's much easier to point out what someone else is doing wrong. But self-reflection is the key to becoming successful and fulfilled in this life. Let me explain.

My relationship with my divorced parents was strained during my childhood. Once I went off to college it didn't get any better, potentially worse. After graduating from college, I still felt a lot of anger and resentment towards them. But one day, with the help of my best friend at the time, I analyzed the root of the strain in these very important relationships. And while it was easy to point the finger at each parent and detail their every wrong move, I was an adult and my role needed to be examined. I learned that I wasn't very forgiving. And while I was always doing my best to be respectful to my parents in tone and attitude, I wasn't very loving, because I was holding a grudge. How could our relationship improve and become loving, if I was short with them and resentful towards them every time we talked? Inside I was actually very angry at them both and it made every encounter tense and uncomfortable. They had both moved on from the past, but I was still holding on to hurt.

I had to step back and realize that I was part of the problem. Many people refuse to see their role in the problem. They think it has nothing to do with them and it's totally the other party's fault. Unfortunately, not being self-aware only compounds this problem because you don't even know to analyze your role. You could be the problem.

I knew of a colleague who changed jobs frequently. There was always a problem with her boss or coworkers. After about the third move in three years, I wondered what the real problem was. Then when I had to work with this colleague on a project, I quickly realized she didn't accept other ideas or their feedback on her work. She quickly became defensive and confrontational. She was unaware of her own behavior and how it made for a hostile environment and frankly an unhappy life for herself.

Don't be the person that can be told nothing and views everyone else as the problem. So how could my coworker turn things around? By being self-aware and improving the traits that are damaging to relationships.

Personality Trait Assessment

The goal of this activity is to get experience taking and analyzing a personality test (adapted from Kacher, D., http://www.quia.com/pages/dkacher/page32). Self-awareness is key if you aim to succeed in your personal and professional life. I hope that once you take a personality test you will have a much better understanding of who you are and your natural tendencies. You can then understand the people not like you much more clearly and uncover a much easier and more effective way to interact and communicate with those people.

There are many different personality trait assessments available online that are used in corporate environments. Once you learn how to read and understand a person's personality, you will have a competitive advantage in understanding the most effective way to communicate with them.

Most people answer the questions the way they wish they were, as opposed to the way they really are. So be careful not to do that. By getting an honest personality assessment score, you can best use the information provided. Remember this is for personal growth.

Do not take a great deal of time with each question. It should take you less than ten minutes to take the full test. You will score most accurately if you go with your initial reaction to each question instead of over-analyzing each one.

Instructions

For each row, circle the one word or phrase you identify with most, the word that best describes you or your preferences at this moment in time. Take the test honestly. Don't choose the phrase you think you should be. When you've completed that page, circle the corresponding colors on the Tally Sheet. For example: if you circle sensitive on line 1 of the test page, circle blue on the tally sheet. Once you complete the tally sheet, total the individual colors.

Assessment

1.	Self-confident	Structure	Sensitive	Trusting
2.	Spontaneous	Checks with others	Dreamer	Analytical
3.	Likes involvement	Likes organization	Likes being straightforward	Likes to explore
4.	Stubborn	Dictatorial	Rebellious	Easily offended
5.	Demanding	Nurturing	Persistent	Quiet
6.	Joiner	Likes to brainstorm	Resists change	Takes charge
7.	Cautious	Overgenerous	Harmonious	Energic
8.	Caring	Outspoken	Steadfast behavior	Mild-mannered
9.	Believable	Forceful	Disciplined	Possessive
10.	Daring	Idealist	Dutiful	Playful
11.	Logical	Contented	Friendly	Bold
12.	Eager	Imaginative	Accurate	Well-liked
13.	Reserved	Inventive	Charismatic	Optimistic
14.	Authoritative	Team worker	Independent	Conservative
15.	Talkative	Restless	Conscientious	Modest
16.	Leader	Counselor	Designer	Controller
17.	Meticulous	Workaholic	Supportive	Self-directed

18.	Industrious	Attentive to details	Prolific mental imager	Positive thinker
19.	Task-oriented	People-oriented	Idea-oriented	Result-oriented
20.	Emotional	Flexible	Likes recognition	Particular
21.	Irritable	Rigid	Easily slighted	Easily threatened
22.	Indirect	Frank	Careful	Strict
23.	Goal-oriented	Capable	Volunteers for tasks	Schedule-oriented
24.	Excels in emergencies	Thrives on compliments	Dry sense of humor	Avoids causing attention
25.	Enjoys watching people	Strong-willed	Enthusiastic	Sets high standards
26.	Very self-confident	Cautiously makes friends	Likes to be thorough	Trendy dresser
27.	Tidy	Looks good	Avoids conflict	Usually right

Tally Sheet

1.	Red	Green	Blue	Yellow
2.	Red	Yellow	Blue	Green
3.	Yellow	Green	Red	Red
4.	Green	Red	Yellow	Blue
5.	Red	Yellow	Green	Blue
6.	Yellow	Blue	Green	Red
7.	Green	Blue	Yellow	Red
8.	Yellow	Red	Green	Blue
9.	Yellow	Red	Green	Blue
10.	Red	Blue	Green	Yellow
11.	Green	Blue	Yellow	Red
12.	Red	Blue	Green	Yellow
13.	Green	Blue	Red	Yellow
14.	Red	Yellow	Blue	Green
15.	Yellow	Red	Green	Blue
16.	Red	Yellow	Blue	Green
17.	Green	Red	Yellow	Blue
18.	Red	Green	Blue	Yellow
19.	Green	Yellow	Blue	Red
20.	Blue	Yellow	Red	green
21.	Red	Green	Blue	Yellow
22.	Yellow	Red	Blue	Green
23.	Red	Blue	Yellow	Green
24.	Red	Yellow	Blue	Green
25.	Blue	Red	Yellow	Green
26.	Red	Blue	Green	Yellow
27.	Green	Yellow	Blue	Red

Talley up the number of each color:

Red _____

Blue _____

Green _____

Yellow_____

Let's reflect on what you have learned through your personality assessment. What is your dominant color? You may even have a two-way tie. Here are the colors and common characteristics:

RED

Red personality types tend to make good leaders because they are results-oriented, thrive in leadership roles and are great delegators. They love being recognized and considered the leader or the boss. They are confident and are often the first to speak up.

YELLOW

Yellow personality types are people oriented and very friendly. They love being around people and participating in team sports. They are great at keeping groups together because they are fun loving. They are often a talkative bunch.

GREEN

Green personality types like order, attention to detail, and like to do things right the first time. They are perceived as the "neat freaks" because of their precision traits, make efficient treasurers and secretaries. They like to keep the team on track.

BLUE

Blue personality types are perceived as quiet or the shyer of all the colors. They are innovative and creative people who like the arts. They enjoy being alone and free thinking.

Now that you've analyzed yourself against the color traits, answer these questions.

What have you learned about yourself?

I make good treasurers and secretaries
I'm aware of my "neat freak" traits

Why might more than one red personality type in a group lead to conflict?

each want to lead — similar traits

Why do you think yellow personality types need a red or green group member to keep them on task?

people oriented, get distracted and need structure
and guidance

How can you better communicate with blue personality types?

Keep them engaged
develop good communication lines

Now that you know the colors and what behaviors may be present in yourself and others you communicate with, think about how you can improve your communications with others.

New Habit

Regular Reflection: Take time, every few days, to reflect on specific situations that have occurred (meetings you attended, conversations with family members, etc.). How did things go? What went well? What didn't go well? What traits did you portray to the other party's involved? What could you have done differently?

Cease Toxic Behavior

What behavior(s) do you need to stop doing to move forward successfully? Bad habits can be broken but it takes willpower and prayer. Where there is a will there is a way!

When and what are the circumstances under which you do the behavior?

high expectations
demanding
perfectionism
critical

Write down what you feel when you do the bad habit.

Stressed
irritable

Replace that habit with another activity. Write three potential substitute behaviors (stop the undesirable activity and start writing, remind yourself of why you need to stop, meditate, call an accountability partner, etc.).

acceptance
be ok with different ways
ask for help → delegate and be ok

Reflection

How do you feel about your relationships? Do you have a strategy to repair strained relationships? Use the space below to map out your plans to have healthier and happier relationships.

I feel good — released toxic relationships
work on maintaining & strenghthening supportive ones

2 Increase Your Self-esteem

Mantra

I am happy, healthy, and hopeful. I am worth it.

Challenge

Approach three people today, introduce yourself and ask them what they like to do for fun.

Quote

> *"Don't allow anybody to make you feel like you are nobody."* — *Martin Luther King, Jr.*

Objectives

1. Contrast confidence, self-esteem, and self-motivation

2. Start a self-esteem journal and a gratitude journal

3. Bring the Law of Attraction into your daily life

Confidence

I wouldn't be where I am if I lacked confidence. Confidence is *a feeling of self-assurance arising from one's appreciation of one's own abilities or qualities* (Oxford dictionary). Confidence is the belief in your ability to do something based on your own unique qualities. Could a daughter of teen parents who grew up in a lower socioeconomic background become a researcher and professor that teaches America's future business leaders? Not if she lacked confidence. I'm proud that my family encouraged me to go as far as I could in life. I realize not everyone has that type of emotional support and if you fall into that category, it's important for you to build those positive influences within yourself.

Self-esteem

Growing up I was thin. It was a genetic trait passed down to me and there was nothing I could eat to change that. And unfortunately, kids are cruel, and I was teased and bullied about it. By the time I was in 8th grade, I was wearing two pairs of pants hoping I would look heavier than I actually was. I can't believe the measures I went through to look heavier! Once I got on fire about going to college, other's negative opinions of me had less weight. Literally. I was focused on having a rich and satisfying life. I had a vision that one day I would travel the world and see Tahiti, Paris, and Hawaii. That I would live a stable life full of purpose and enjoyment. Visualizing myself traveling the world gave me such hope and I began to develop confidence in myself!

There is a great deal of self-esteem required to have personal confidence so let's start there. Self-esteem reflects your subjective attitude and opinion of your worth. Those suffering from depression often have a low self-esteem. The happiest and most successful people have high self-esteem. Psychology Today reports that possessing little self-regard can lead people to become depressed, to fall short of their potential or to tolerate abusive situations and relationships (Psychologytoday.com/basics/self-esteem).

Self-motivation

What is the one thing that you want to see happen in your life? What's your biggest dream come true? Don't downplay your idea. Shoot for the stars!

to be happy
not stress about money
have strong relationships with friends and family

Focusing on this big dream will help you become more self-motivated. Think about it, if you have nothing important or meaningful to work towards, then you won't be very motivated.

Something special happens when you believe that what you desire is possible. But you first must believe. Speak it into existence and it will happen. It may not happen when you want it to. It took me years to apply to a Ph.D. graduate program due to some obstacles, but I was admitted the first time I applied. Believe it and speak it into the atmosphere!

New Habit: Self-esteem journal

I love writing in my gratitude journal. Each night I reflect on what God is doing in my life and what I am grateful for. Even if I am feeling low, tired or just blue, writing in my journal improves my mood. Things could be worse and writing down what I am grateful for helps me to remember that things aren't so bad. And when things are terrible, I remember the only thing I can change is my attitude about it. Use the template below to start a gratitude journal.

·Gratitude and Self-esteem Journal·

	MONDAY
Today I felt proud when…	I didn't stress about last minute tasks
I am thankful for…	my health and family
	TUESDAY
Today I accomplished…	rush work assignment
I helped someone…	Ani with setting up her new bed
	WEDNESDAY
I like that I am…	at peace
I am proud that…	I can acknowledge my mistakes + negative thoughts
	THURSDAY
Today I was inspired when…	I'm focused on getting life in order + being healthy
I know that I can…	continue to improve + manage emotions
	FRIDAY
Today I did good when…	
I am good at…	
	SATURDAY
_____…	
_____…	
	Sunday
_____…	
_____…	

Reflection

How do you feel about your self-esteem?

I still have low self-esteem and trying to focus on me.

What do you need to improve on?

Spending
Exercise Routine

What motivates you?

When I'm organized
cooking

Write three actions you will take this week to be happier with yourself.

Start exercise routine - 10 minute morning
journaling
Eating healthy snacks

3 Define Your Passion & Purpose

Mantra

There is a purpose for my life. I was here.

(YouTube the video of the song, *I Was Here*, by Beyoncé.)

Challenge

If you could share one message with the world, what would it be? Share this message with someone you trust. Believe

Quote

"The reason I've been able to be so financially successful is my focus has never, ever for one minute, been money." — Oprah Winfrey

Objectives

1. Decipher talent from passion

2. Determine your life purpose

3. Write your life mission statement

Talent vs Passion

I'll never forget the day I sat in a high school business class as a teacher observation assignment for one of my education courses while enrolled in college. I was majoring in business information systems business education. I was a sophomore and it was my first time observing a teacher. She was lively, happy and engaged with her students. The students were hanging on to her every word and when she assigned them to small groups to work, they happily obliged and got right down to business. She walked around to check their work and give feedback. On several occasions, I heard that sweet "Ahhh now I get it" and high fives smacking in the air. I was amazed and thought to myself, that's the kind of teacher I want to be. But over the next couple of years my business and information systems classes became more interesting and I dropped the education minor and focused on corporate America. But I longed to be a teacher. My professors encouraged me to first get corporate experience and then consider a Doctor of Philosophy degree.

My Talent

During my junior year of college, I landed an internship in the finance department of a Fortune 100 corporation. I had interviewed for an IT internship but was offered one in finance. Which was still perfect because I got my foot in the door at one of the world's best companies, Caterpillar Financial Corporation. I was really good in my information systems classes and had a natural knack for information technology. My senior year, I interviewed for a full-time position at the same Fortune 100 company and was offered a full-time position in the Information Technology department.

My time at the company was full of growth and opportunity. My natural ability to learn fast and communicate well allowed me to advance quickly, but each night I felt that something was missing. I still had the desire to teach.

My Passion

One day I checked the mail and found a postcard from The PhD Project. It was an invitation to apply to their annual conference to learn about applying and obtaining a Ph.D. degree. Was this a sign from God? Turns out that it was a sign for me to pursue a doctorate degree. I attended the conference the next year in 2003. I applied and was accepted to the University of Mississippi in 2007 and graduated in 2011.

I am honored to motivate, empower and teach future business leaders in management information systems classes. My classes are experiential and lively just like the business school teacher who once inspired me. I'm thankful that I get to use my talents while living my passion.

I'm also a women's rights activist and humanitarian. This is where I receive my greatest rewards. Out of my love for empowering women, I founded The Achiever Academy. The Achiever Academy is a mentoring and leadership organization to develop poised, persistent, and prosperous young women through personal and professional development experiences. The Academy hosts fine dining and service experiences that include leadership events and soft skills workshops focused on three outcomes: career success, community impact, and a prosperous life.

With the help of our college AchieveHers we give back in a big way. On March 8, 2018, to commemorate International Women's Day, we held an all-girls school assembly to empower over 200 high school students to stay in school, graduate, and achieve their long-term goals. The empowerment session began with me asking them Beyoncé's famous question, "who run the world?" And the immediate response was "GIRLS!" It only got better from there. There were serious moments and laughter but by the end of it, they walked away with their goal plan for the rest of the year and big purple tote bag filled with a month's supply of period products. I will never forget the feeling I had that day. I have never felt so accomplished. I knew right then why I am here. From then on, period news followed me! I was contacted by the Tennessean newspaper to talk about period poverty and the impact on girls in middle Tennessee. The community outpouring from the electronic article was overwhelming and I knew I had to galvanize the community around this issue. I was in New Orleans speaking at the PhD Project conference the day the article was published in the newspaper. The next morning, my significant other and I were having breakfast at our favorite New Orleans restaurant when I had a brilliant idea. I said, "wouldn't it be great if we could do a city-wide donation drive for a full month?"

He replied, "Babe, I think that is a great idea and you should do it throughout the month of September."

I said, "It probably won't work, I don't know enough people to pull it off."

He said, "Okay, but I bet you'll be doing the drive in September." Later that night, I received a Facebook direct message from an elected official asking if I'd like to do a press conference on period poverty and that's when I sprang into action. I asked them if they'd like to partner on my city-wide donation challenge and the rest is history. We ended up being in the newspaper again, on several radio stations, and speaking at events across the city to raise awareness. The citizens and organizations donated over 200,000 products to the Metropolitan Nashville Public School district! Wow!

Passion: What makes you come alive? Visualize then describe the situation by answering what, when, where, who, why.

Cooking
Dancing
Crafty
Running
Organizing

_____

_____

Talent: What are you naturally good at? Remember, we often believe everyone is good at the same things we are. But that simply isn't true. So, list those talents that you possess that come naturally to you.

organizing ~ crafts
cooking
music - dancing - arts
running

Now complete the *My Life Purpose* worksheet to dive deeper into your life purpose and start to live it.

My Life Purpose Worksheet

If money was no object, I would...	travel more and spend time exploring intensely attend art events — go to school culinary classes
Describe your ideal day. What will you do?	exercise, eat right, complete tasks planned self-care, read
What would you like people at your funeral to say about you?	I was caring and brought a positive difference in their life.
Who is someone you aspire to emmulate?	? someone who is happy in their life, by helping others — been watching youtubers incorporating Plant-based diet
If I could solve a world problem, it would be...	nutrition — eliminate obesity starving children
I am really good at __ but my passion is	my job passion — incorporating a healthy lifestyle
Review your answers. List 3 life purposes and your next steps.	Retirement Travel/hobbies healthy life style

Mission Statement

So, what's your mission? Writing a mission or purpose statement gives your life a destination. You will feel more grounded and that your life has meaning. First, review all your work in this chapter and think about your true mission in life. A mission statement is a concise way of explaining an organization's purpose, goals, and overall intention. A mission statement explains what you do and supports a vision. It clarifies the what (we do) and who (is affected). Here are a few examples:

Oprah Winfrey: To be a teacher. And to be known for inspiring my students to be more than they thought they could be.

The PhD Project: To increase the diversity of corporate America by increasing the diversity of business school faculty.

The Achiever Academy: To support, mentor and teach young adult women to be poised, persistent, and prosperous through sophisticated and inspiring experiences.

Write a personal mission statement for yourself. Be concise, 5-20 words is the average length of most mission statements.

To live a happy, healthy life.
To spend more time with family.
Develop meaningful friendship
Travel
Allocate time for hobbies
Utilize talents to help others

Personal Vision Statement

A vision statement paints the picture of your ideal future and describes your desired outcome. If we've lived our mission and accomplished that work, the vision is the result. I have been creating and revising my own mission statement for years. Here are a few examples:

The PhD Project: A significantly larger pool of highly qualified African-Americans, Hispanic-Americans, and Native Americans for positions in management.

The Achiever Academy: Young adult women are highly achieved, poised, persistent, and prosperous in their personal and professional lives.

Write a personal vision statement for yourself. Again, be clear and as concise as possible.

A happier healthier lifestyle that supports & is supported by family, friends and giving back to the community.

Reflection

Flip back through this chapter. Think about how your thinking and mindset have changed. Write down your feelings about where your passion lies and your purpose on earth.

I have a vision but it's hard to get inspired and motivated.

4 Using Body Language

Mantra

My poise speaks for me before I ever say a word.

Challenge

Take this body language quiz:

1. What do leaders do?

   A: Smile more ✓

B: Smile less

2. What do leaders do?

   A. Pace

B. Stand Still ✓

3. What do leaders do?

   A. Nod as you speak to them. ✓

B. Hold their head still as you speak to them.

Answers: 1. B, 2. B, 3. B

Quote

> *"Shoes transform your body language and attitude. They*
> *lift you physically and emotionally."*
> — *Christian Louboutin.*

Objectives

1. Learn to interpret body language

2. Use intentional body language

3. What to wear

4. What to say

5. Practice dining etiquette

Have you ever met someone with a natural magnetism and as soon as they walk in the room everyone pauses? Someone whose confidence and poise are so powerful that everyone wants to engage with them? Maybe that person is you? If this isn't you already, it can be.

This chapter will prepare you to communicate effectively in personal and professional environments. I am going to share with you the seven most impactful body language and social networking tips every woman should know. We are constantly sending and receiving messages through our words, tone, and body language. Look around for the Alpha in the room. The Alpha is usually the most dominant person in the room. Let's begin with how leaders project their confidence and power.

How to interpret another persons body language

This is the section you really want to master. Later I will give you many poses and stances to use to invoke specific feelings from your audience. However, you cannot interpret a single pose as fact, unless you have taken time to first build rapport with a person and understand their natural tendencies. For example, let's say you are in a negotiation and you are trying to interpret the other party's body language. How do you know if what they are saying is genuine or a lie? If you don't take time to first understand their natural behavior, then you won't know when they get uncomfortable, change and begin being untruthful. Does this person usually look at the floor or ceiling when they talk to someone or do they begin that once the conversation gets uncomfortable. These clues help you identify when someone is no longer comfortable and possibly crafting their words or speaking untrue. Use this information in your own body language communication. Be careful that your body language doesn't change too drastically when switch from speaking about non-stressful topics to more uncomfortable topics. I highly recommend the book, *You Say More than You Think*, (Janine Driver, 2011) to learn more about body language and baselines. Janine is a retired FBI agent and teaches body language all over the world.

How to project power and confidence when speaking

Now that we've discussed the interpretation of body language, let's talk about more power strategies in body language. The most viral and electric TED Talks have speakers who spoke with their words and hands. When using your hand gestures, keep them close to your body in front of you, never above your shoulders or your hands could become a distraction. See the images below. Wild arms can be a distraction and cause your audience to look at your hands more than focusing in on your emotion and story. Figure 1 is a good representation of hand use. However, be careful not to be too wild (as in figure 2) nor too stiff (figure 3). Be expressive, but not distracting.

Figure 1. Good body language   Figure 2. Distracting body language

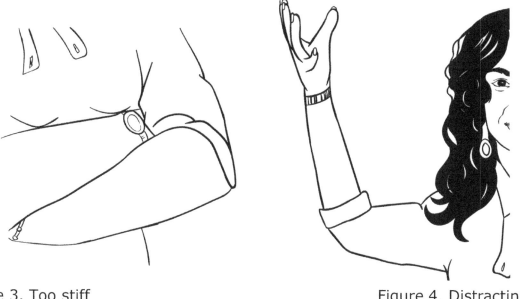

Figure 3. Too stiff   Figure 4. Distracting

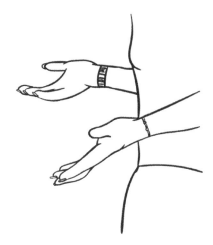

Figure 5. Expressive and welcoming

Look and act interested (where are your feet facing?)

I can't stress the importance of looking interested even if you are not. People remember those who seemed interested in what they had to say. Show you are an intense listener by <u>turning your head, feet, and torso to face them directly</u>. Face your feet toward to the front of the person you are speaking to. When you

41

position your feet and body right in front of the person you are speaking to, they'll feel you're interested in what they have to say. <u>Leaning forward and slightly nodding</u> every now and again shows you are listening. Don't nod too much or you can seem submissive. Also, <u>a slight touch to your chin</u> demonstrates that you are paying close attention and thinking about what the speaker is saying.

Shake hands to make an instant connection

Touching someone for as little as 1/40 of a second creates a human bond. A study on handshakes by the Income Center for Trade Shows showed that people are two times more likely to remember you if you shake hands with them. (Carol Kinsey Goman, Ph.D. http://www.amanet.org/training/articles/10-powerful-body-language-tips.aspx)

Steepling

This is a commonly used gesture to exude confidence and superiority. Bring your hands up in front of your chest and the tips of your fingertips together. Use it during interviews and meetings you are leading or when engaging in one on one meetings, conversations or networking events.

Mirroring

Rapport building is an important first step in any relationship. Research has shown that when you mirror other people, you are building rapport by nursing feelings of mutuality. Start by observing the other person's body gestures and then mirror those gestures. People like people similar to them and when you mirror, you make the other person feel understood and accepted (Carol Kinsey Goman, Ph.D. http://www.amanet.org/training/articles/10-powerful-body-language-tips.aspx).

Seem approachable and open

If you want to be seen as open with nothing to hide, try the hands behind your back position. Put your hands behind your back and grab one wrist. Spread your feet so each foot is under your shoulder. This is a common politician pose that is used by those who are confident. You'll also see teachers use this position as they walk around a classroom.

If you are at a networking event and have a plate or cup in your hand, make sure it is not forming a barrier between you and others. Hold the cup or saucer low around your waist and off to the side of your body, not in front except to drink, of course. And remember to smile, but not too much. Smiling too much can make you seem immature and passive.

Overall, just remember to be engaging, interested and keep your body relaxed and unguarded. Crossing your arms and feet can have a negative feeling to others. Create space with your body. Feet should be shoulder width apart and arms loose.

What to wear

Basic business colors are black, blue, grey and brown. You are safe with these solid colors. When going for power and confidence, you will often see more power players in black and red. According to *Science of People* (https://www.scienceofpeople.com/body-language-alphas-nonverbal-secrets-leader/), black is the color of mystery and power, while red is the color of aggression, passion, and violence. You often see politicians wear black suits with red ties. Blue ties may be worn, and this is because blue is the color of wisdom, loyalty, and honesty.

Let's talk shoes. We love the look of a professional pump or sleek high heel. But the feeling isn't so nice after a few hours at a networking event or working on your feet all day. Keep the size of the shoe heel in mind when planning your wardrobe for a special event. You don't want your body to scream "my feet hurt."

Daily, you want to work in what you feel good wearing. Some women prefer heels and others prefer flats. I have a good friend who wears heels while she will be networking because since she's shorter than average. Heels make her taller and it's easier to network when she's two inches taller. Be careful when wearing heels higher than two inches as they can look unprofessional.

What to say

Networking events can come in many forms: dinners, lunches, conferences, or even receptions. Knowing how to quickly connect, and make a memorable impact is key in these environments. Try to find a similarity you two can connect on. Are you in the same field? Do they volunteer with similar organizations? Did you go to school in the same area? That will make the interaction memorable. Remember the traffic light strategy from *NPR* radio host Marty Nemko (https://www.fastcompany.com/3052732/how-to-figure-out-what-to-say-at-networking-events):

Green light: the first 20 seconds your listener is engaged in what you are saying.

Yellow light: during the next 20 seconds you risk the other person losing interest or think you're becoming long-winded.

Red light: at the 40-second mark, you need to turn the conversation over to the other person by asking them an engaging open-ended question.

Often, the difference between getting a job or an opportunity comes from relationships with the right people. Remember, try to find a similarity you two can connect on. Use these three steps to find that similarity.

1. Break the ice. Look approachable and show genuine interest by using the body language tips from above. Then, when you meet someone new, start the conversation with an open-ended *relevant* question that is all about breaking the ice with a person.

Pick two questions from below to be your go-to questions:

"Is this the first time you've been to this meeting?"

"How long have you been involved with this organization?"

"How do you know the host?"

"I'm looking forward to the speaker. Have you ever heard her?"

"How can we get more females involved in this?"

Respond with a matching statement directly to their response. For example, if they say, "This is my first time and I'm not sure what to expect," you can say, "Yes, it can be a little intimidating."

2. Build rapport and sell your elevator pitch. Next, ask a personal question that causes the other person to tell you their story/elevator pitch. Some great go-to questions are:

"How long have you lived in this city?

"What kind of work do you do?"

"What have you been working on lately?"

Then be prepared to reciprocate. This is your opportunity to tell your story. An elevator pitch is about a 30-second description of your expertise and credentials. Some people say 30 seconds but, in my experience, (and according to the stop light rules above) people get bored after about 20 seconds. You will be fine at 30 seconds for your elevator speech but make it compelling! Then, you can move into personal questions that go into a conversation (keep replies brief to keep the conversation moving deeper). Here is an example elevator pitch:

I recently graduated from college with a degree in entrepreneurship. I worked on the college DECA team, and eventually, as the team captain. I started a fashion line for women called, AchieveHer Fashions. I'm looking for investors for my new fashion line.

I'm a business professor of information systems. My research expertise is in data mining and analytics and my passion is equipping and empowering women for success. I founded The Achiever Academy, a mentoring and leadership academy for college females and the Homework Suite Reminder app for all students to track their homework. I'm currently seeking support for my book tour.

Prepare your draft elevator pitch below.

I'm a staff services manager I for the CDPH.
I have a team/staff of 3 that is responsible for the processing involving payment of all the over 400 contracts in the CA division.
Currently, I am redirected to Std to assist in their BCP + PRA processes.
The strengths + skills that help me succeed my job are my organization skills, attention to detail, innovative ideas, responsibility + commitment, to get things done — I enjoy fostering a positive work environment, pride, developing staff, and streamlining processes.

Now film yourself.

Film yourself chatting with someone on the phone. You might be surprised what gestures you use and how many you use during the conversation. Then, film yourself delivering your elevator pitch. Have a friend give you feedback on your gestures.

3. Find a match and offer help. Remember, it's not only about what you want out of the relationship. Dig deep to find something you both enjoy and/or are engaged with. Getting to know the other party can help you identify how you can help them with their goals. People also like to talk about themselves. How can I help you? This is a killer question that catches most mentors off guard. Most mentees are only concerned about what they can take from a mentor. When you communicate that you are genuinely willing to give, you will set yourself miles apart from everyone else. Who doesn't like a win/win relationship?

4. Shake hands and politely end the conversation. Too often someone at a networking event capitalizes too much of your time. Before you know it, you've spent 10 minutes or more with one person. This is fine if you've found someone interesting and you know you are creating an opportunity for future collaboration or support. If the connection is there, continue to go deeper and set a future date to meet up again. But you really must move on and work the room.

A good rule of thumb is about 5 minutes per person, or shorter if you couldn't find a matching point or connection and more time if you've really connected. But at some point, the conversation must end.

If things went well and you are genuinely interested in speaking with this person more, plan a follow up.

"I would love to speak more. Can I have your card and contact you to arrange a meeting?"

If you don't know that you have anything further to discuss, wait for a natural pause in the conversation and then say something like:

"I don't want to take up all your time, it was great chatting with you."

Or

"I'm going to grab a bite to eat, but I enjoyed chatting with you."

In summary, your body language communicates as much as your verbal communication and it's a good idea to practice your poses and posture along with your speech.

Review the section on *"What to Say"*. Now write down one question from each part that will be your go-to question:

Break the ice.

How long have you worked at CDPH?

Build Rapport

What kind of work do you do?

Find a match

How can I help you?

End the conversation

I look forward to working with you at the training.

Dining etiquette

Along with appropriate body language comes appropriate dining etiquette. Study this sheet to be prepared for your next luncheon or business meeting.

Soup

Be sure to use a soup spoon. Hold the spoon with the handle on your middle finger, with your thumb on top.

To eat, skim the spoon away from you and sip from the side of the spoon. When you get to the end, slightly tip the bowl away from you to scoop the last spoonful.

Utensils

1) Hold your fork in your left hand, tines downward.
2) Hold your knife in your right hand.
3) Use your fork to spear bite-sized food and lift it to your mouth.
4) Utensils stay on your plate once they have been used.
5) Eat from the outside utensils inward.
6) Remember BMW from the left. Your bread plate is on the left, meal in the middle, and water on your right.

When to Start Eating

If you are joined by a small party of two to four people, wait until everyone else been served before starting to eat. Except when at a formal or business meal, then you should wait until everyone is served or when the host announces that you may now enjoy your meal.

Passing

1) Pass food counterclockwise, or to the right. When a guest asks for something specific on the table, you may pass it in their direction.

2) Always pass the salt and pepper together!

Seating

Host   Hostess
Guest of Honor

Bread

1) Use the cloth in the bread basket to maneuver the bread to the piece you want or to hold the bread to cut it.

2) Place the bread and butter on your butter plate. Tear off a bite-sized piece of bread and butter it right before you eat it.

New Habit

Memorize your favorite questions above and practice using them daily. There is always an opportunity to meet someone new and build a new relationship that may prove fruitful. Don't forget the importance of steeling and watching the body language of others to decipher what's really being said.

Reflection

What surprised you about what you learned about your own body language habits? About your dining etiquette? What is your main take away from this chapter?

_____
_____
_____
_____
_____
_____

Persistence

5 Overcome Obstacles And Be Happy

Mantra

I can jump any hurdle and overcome any obstacle.

Challenge

On a slip of paper, write the one thing you need to overcome and put behind you. Pray or meditate and release the item from your consciousness. Light a candle and burn the paper to represent the evaporation of the obstacles. Let it burn. *Fear of heights*

Quote

forgive those who tramatically hurt me

> *"All the struggle will one day explode into your moment of success. Don't quit." — Dr. Kisha Simmons*

Objectives

1. Build courage to overcome obstacles

2. Let go of the past

3. Move forward

4. The courage to overcome obstacles

Obstacles get in our way and keep us from being happy and prosperous. Sometimes you may think you are not meant to be happy. Well, that isn't true! You can and will be happy. Let's get to work.

Rule number one for a happy and successful life, don't make excuses for yourself. I'm sorry, but nobody wants to hear all about the negative things happening in your life. Can they fix it? Likely not. But you can. So, if you must tell someone about your challenges, always follow-up with a positive statement. This will change your outlook and attitude.

I heard a story of a young lady whose mother abandoned her at an early age. The young lady used that as an excuse for why she didn't go to college (didn't have family to use on a FASFA) and why she couldn't make enough money to pay her bills (wasn't taught money management). You see, everything this lady is going through is her mother's fault. But unfortunately, whether it's her mother's fault or not doesn't matter. It's about having the courage to overcome the wrong done to you and move onward and upward successfully.

In middle school, I lived with my aunt. That time in my life was very dark because I honestly didn't feel like my mother or father wanted me. I felt like an outsider in my aunt's house and soon shuffled to another family member's house. They had little, but they took me in and cared for me unconditionally. They even took me on a college tour to support my dream of going to college. The last semester of my senior year in high school I moved back with my mother and we attempted a relationship again. While our relationship is much better today, it was strained for some time. I don't aim to hurt anyone's feelings, but this is my truth. I've seen a lot and experienced bouts of depression and anxiety throughout my life. What I know to be true is that no one controls my happiness but me (there are chemicals in our body we don't control - more on that in the Anxiety chapter). I can overcome my circumstances and still rise to the top. With faith and courage, I can do anything.

We've done work on our self-esteem and confidence, now let's build courage. We won't have the strength to overcome obstacles without courage. What is courage? Courage is the ability to continue in the midst of fear, pain or grief. Courage can be taught young, so we can stand up when we are older. The best example is having the courage to get back on the bike once you've fallen off and hurt yourself.

One of my favorite ways to build courage is to surround myself with friends who are brave and have high self-esteem. I also encourage others to take more risks. Put forth more ideas in classes or meetings. Challenge yourself to initiate more conversations in networking environments. Practice is the best way to build courage. You can even role play in front of a mirror to build courage.

Do you ever run from your problems, make excuses for poor decisions, procrastinate on your life's goals? Let's brainstorm how you would overcome these obstacles:

Your child is being bullied in school. What do you tell him or her?

Be confident and confront bully to stand up for self

Your best friend is being skipped over for a promotion. What do you tell him or her?

To obtain feedback and focus on improving self.
by developing, refining skills.

Now it's your turn to look inward. List your fears in each category. List the things you are afraid to do and brainstorm how you can overcome them.

fear, lack of motivation

self confidence

phobias

anxiety

4 things you must give up to move forward

To reach your goals you must be self-disciplined and goal driven. We all struggle with forgiving our past or circumstances. Accept the past, then complete the boxes below to begin moving forward.

Excuses		Avoidance	
Why do I make excuses?	_fear, not motivated_	Why do I avoid important things?	_complicated_
Obstacles I need to overcome...	_lack of motivation_	Obstacles I need to overcome...	_unknown_
Action I will take...	_small goals_	Action I will take...	_face fears_

Shame		_fear_ Name your own obstacle to overcome	
Why do I feel shame?	_concerned of perception_	Why do I _fear_ ?	_anxiety unknown_
Obstacles I need to overcome...	_self confidence_	Obstacles I need to overcome...	_anxiety →_
Action I will take...	_self affirmations_	Action I will take...	_self-care_

New Habits

One trick to overcoming your obstacles is to visualize your future situation. Close your eyes and meditate on being in that moment when you reach your ultimate goals. Here are some ways you can be reminded about your future.

1. Look at your goals daily on paper (vision board, a statement, a quote etc.).

2. Write them on your bathroom mirror.

3. Change your phone screen saver to a photo of your vision board or a saying or quote that motivates you.

Reflection

Review your mantra: I can jump any hurdle and overcome any obstacle.

Now take a few moments to close your eyes and take three deep breaths. Relax your shoulders and calm your mind. Slowly open your eyes and write down your feelings about overcoming your obstacles or fears. Do you feel encouraged? Why or why not? Is there anything else holding you back?

_____

_____

_____

_____

_____

_____

_____

_____

6 Conflict Resolution

Mantra

I create strategies to break through any conflict.

Challenge

Think about the last time you walked away from a situation feeling unsatisfied. Did you leave feeling you left something on the table or that you got the bad end of the deal? Write down what you felt in that moment and what you felt went wrong.

> Recently - delegated mother's day —
> i restated what was agreed and left it
> leaving it alone without follow up left me unsatisfied.
> don't think it's wrong an it's necessary
> I am focused only on my agreed task and shifting
> focus to other activities

Quote

"Everything is negotiable. Whether the
negotiation is easy is another thing."
— Carrie Fisher

Objectives

1. Define conflict and discuss what you need to solve it
2. Discuss effective communications for successful change
3. Identify successful negotiation techniques
4. Conflict resolution and negotiation

Conflict resolution and negotiation go hand in hand because we often must compromise to solve a conflict. If we are effective negotiators, each party can walk away with something they want. It doesn't always have to be a winner and a loser. But you must have two parties willing to communicate and come to an agreement. In my experience, people focus too much on one thing they want and don't focus on what the root need is or evaluate all avenues to get there.

We've all experienced conflict sometimes in our lives. Conflict is simply the disagreement between ideas, principles, commitment or objectives. We experience conflict in the workplace, among friends and even in our homes. Here are some of the major causes of conflict:

- Poor attitude

- No buy in / challenge to values

- Unmet needs

- Desire for power

- Ignorance

- Cultural threat

- Self-interest

Attitude and emotions

So how do we solve it? Begin by having a positive and reasonable attitude. Many conflicts lead to an emotional response which might be anger or hurt. Before you can begin to resolve, you must put the emotions aside so you can be reasonable. This is difficult to do, and many people don't have the emotional intelligence to do it. But with awareness and practice, it can be done. The best leaders are good at resolving conflict because they first remove any feelings from the situation. Once you strip away the emotions you can start being reasonable and then you can effectively work with others to find a sensible solution. Even if the other party is stuck in their emotions, you'll have the upper hand in negotiations.

What are the causes of conflict in your life?

_____

_____

_____

_____

_____

_____

Negotiation

The main point of negotiation is to come to an agreement with another party that is acceptable to both or all involved.   It is a process to facilitate compromise. From who takes out the garbage to how much money you'll make at your new company, negotiation is everywhere. Conflict resolutions sometimes need savvy negotiation skills. For a simple example, let's say you and a friend always have a difficult time agreeing on where to have dinner.   One technique is to flip a coin and allow the winner to list three restaurant options and the loser must choose one of the three. Then next time you are planning to meet up, the past loser gets to offer three choices.

For major conflicts, you must understand the cause of the emotion. If you don't have clear understanding of the emotions behind the conflict, you can end up in deadlock communication. Be compromising, yet assertive. Sometimes, a communicator can stonewall simply because one party is waiting on the other to say, "I'm sorry."

Negotiation techniques to solve conflicts

Once you have managed your emotions, you are ready to prepare for the communication. Here are a few techniques that have worked well for me throughout my corporate and leadership career:

1. Always speak simply and honestly.

Being upfront and honest builds trust. It also saves a lot of time, so you can get right to the root issues. If you can establish trust, you will have an easier time getting to the outcome you desire.

Use this sentence structure to express your feelings: State the factual event and then the feeling you felt due to the event (John M. Gottman, 2001, *The Seven Principles for Making Marriage Work*). For example:

"When you didn't recognize my work, I felt disappointed." The response to this sentence should always begin with a recognition of the person's feelings.

2. Continue to communicate continuously without breaking down or running.

Have you ever dealt with a runner? A runner is someone who can't handle confrontation and will exit the situation as soon as possible. They will claim nothing is wrong but clearly something is wrong. It's not uncommon for one party to be a runner. Let's face it, addressing conflict is an anxiety-inducing situation. But learning to communicate effectively through tough conversation builds leadership and tough skin. You need this level of leadership skill to overcome obstacles and resolve conflict.

3. Be open and willing to understand the other party's perspective.

At the beginning of the communication, start with the willingness to empathize with the other party and attempt to understand their perspective. Take your opinions out of it for the moment and focus on identifying what the other party needs out of the situation.

4. Recognize your personality color and how it may have affected the conflict.

Refer to your notes on self-awareness and take that knowledge into the conflict resolution or negotiation conversation. Knowing yourself and tendencies will help you be more in control during the negotiations.

5. Adjust your body language accordingly (see the chapter on body language).

Remember, your physical expressions, stance and posture can send strong messages, so go into conversations with a plan for your body communication. Don't underestimate the communication of your body. If you can, negotiate in person. Then you can pick up on body language cues and let the other party talk as much as they want (because they will usually reveal important details). But before the meeting make sure you have identified exactly what you want out of the deal. That way you know if you got a good deal or not. Lastly, always be prepared to walk away if the negotiation is not going in your favor. Don't be afraid to walk away. Tell the other party to think about your offer more but also let them know time is limited.

List a conflict you are currently facing (or most recently faced). Then answer the following questions. Was it due to behaviors, attitudes, or structural issues? How was the conflict handled? What would you have done differently?

_____

_____

_____

_____

_____

_____

_____

_____

New Habit

List three role-model qualities you will emulate to improve your conflict resolution skills.

_____

_____

_____

_____

_____

_____

_____

_____

Reflection

Review your notes from the Self-Awareness chapter. Think about your color and how it impacts you when you work with a team. Learning from that information, use it to answer the following questions.

Three ways I can change my behavior and participation when working with others:

_____

_____

_____

_____

_____

How can I position myself for healthy communication in my relationships to prevent conflict?

_____

_____

_____

_____

_____

_____

_____

_____

Now review the challenge from the beginning of this chapter. Write down how you will handle the conflict the next time a similar conflict occurs.

_____

_____

_____

_____

_____

_____

_____

_____

7 Mental Health & Self Care

Mantra

I'm happy, healthy and nothing worries me.

Challenge

Make a list of 10 things that relax you and make you feel at peace. Be sure to list all 10!

1. _____

2. _____

3. _____

4. _____

5. _____

6. _____

7. _____

8. _____

9. _____

10. _____

Objectives

1. Understand and identify common mental health illnesses

2. How to cope and overcome mental health illnesses

3. Create a self-care plan

Quote

> *"Women in particular need to keep an eye on their physical and mental health, because if we're scurrying to and from appointments and errands, we don't have a lot of time to take care of ourselves. We need to do a better job of putting ourselves higher on our own 'to do' list." — Michelle Obama*

Anxiety and Depression

Mental health affects more people than you might think. Approximately 1 in 5 adults in the U.S. (about 43.8 million), experience mental illness in a given year (Any Mental Illness Among Adults). Approximately 1 in 25 adults in the U.S. experience a serious mental illness in a given year that interferes with or limits one or more major life activities (Serious Mental Illness (SMI) Among Adults).

Sometimes it's temporary and controllable and sometimes it's not. It's important to get to the root cause of what is making you anxious or depressed. You must find the source and work on improving or removing that source of tension in your life. While I am not a doctor and cannot give you medical advice, I can hopefully motivate you to seek the help you may need. This chapter is here to help you identify sources of anxiety and discover a few techniques to destress and bring happiness to your daily life while you get the help you may need.

Worry

At one point in my life I experienced high anxiety and it was virtually uncontrollable. I was suddenly, afraid to fly after flying all over the world. I was afraid to get on an airplane fearing a plane crash or that I wouldn't be able to have enough space to breathe. By the way, there is only a one in 5.4 million chance that your plane will actually crash. (*The Economist* https://www.economist.com/blogs/gulliver/2015/01/air-safety).

But we often worry about more daily things like, "I have the flu and am not in the high-risk group but am I going to die"? Or, "what if I have pneumonia"? I have found that worry can plague you to dire levels of brokenness. The majority of the time we are worried about something that never actually happens. Here is what the Bible says about worry:

Mathew 6:25-27:

25 "Therefore I tell you, do not worry about your life, what you will eat or drink; or about your body, what you will wear. Is not life more than food, and the body more than clothes?

26 Look at the birds of the air; they do not sow or reap or store away in barns, and yet your heavenly Father feeds them. Are you not much more valuable than they?

27 Can any one of you by worrying add a single hour to your life?".

Overwhelmed

Juggling many tasks and responsibilities can make someone feel overwhelmed. Even if these are things you enjoy, doing too much can tax your brain and body. Sometimes we don't realize we are becoming overwhelmed until it is too late. That is why you hear so much about balance. Balancing your work time with relaxation time is important. Plan your relaxation time in advance. Brainstorm a few activities you can plan into your day to reduce anxiety and depression when you lead a hectic life or are feeling overwhelmed.

_____

_____

_____

_____

_____

_____

_____

_____

Toxic relationships

Are you in a relationship that causes you stress and anguish? Some relationships may have natural stressful moments, for example, caring for a child. And in those situations, you create peace around the stressful moments, like soft music, candles, bubble baths. But other adult relationships are more than stressful moments. These can be relationships with friends, family or co-workers. Sometimes a relationship needs healing. You and the other party should sit down and resolve the conflict (see the chapter on conflict resolution and negotiation). If you have tried everything possible, it may be time to release the relationship. That may be difficult to comprehend if it's someone close to you, but is your mental health worth it?

Take a moment and assess personal and professional relationships and decide if they are causing undue stress. On the lines below, list out relationships that cause you stress, rate the amount of stress, and decide your course of action. In the first column, list the names of people with relationships that cause you stress.

In the second column, rate the stress from 1-3 (1 is rare stress and 3 is constant stress). Then decide on a course of action. Action options are:

1. Forgive the person but release the relationship. Choose this option if you experience constant stress and you can honestly say you've tried everything. If you and your boss can no longer work in peace, it may be time to find a new job. If it's a personal relation, you may need to exit the relationship. I once had a friend who I loved dearly. But she was selfish and self-centered. It was always about what she wanted and when. One day I decided the stress of trying to keep her happy was weighing too heavy on my emotions and I had to forgive and release that relationship. There have been relationships in my family I have had to release and luckily, they came back better than before. Sometimes it's a temporary separation and sometimes it's a permanent one.

2. Put a plan in place to overcome the obstacle. If you are not totally at your wit's end, you can attempt to negotiate with the other party and come up with a strategy for moving forward. Be very clear and document how each party is to behave going forward. Then decide on what will happen if the rule is broken.

3. Change your behavior (assuming the other person will not change).

Now assess a few of your current relationships below:

Relationship	Amount of Stress	Action

Let's dig a little deeper and get an overall sense of your well-being and self-care. Complete the worksheet below by assessing each statement from strongly disagree (1) to strongly agree (10). Then, depending on your rating, write an appropriate action to improve in that area.

Self-Care Assessment

> In what areas do I need to take care of myself more?
> Let's take some time to assess your self care. Rate yourself in each of the areas below.
> Then go back through your ratings and complete the last column.

	My well-being	(1 is Strongly Disagree and, 10 is Strongly Agree)	What do I need? What action would raise my score?
1	I feel relaxed..	/ 10	
2	I feel inspired.	/ 10	
3	My life is fun.	/ 10	
4	I am in good physical health.	/ 10	
5	My life is peaceful	/ 10	
6	I feel important.	/ 10	
7	I feel a part of something.	/ 10	
8	I have good relationships.	/ 10	
9	I have good physical appearance.	/ 10	
10	I feel loved and appreciated.	/ 10	
11	I have high energy levels.	/ 10	
12	I feel happy.	/ 10	
13	Other: _____	/ 10	

Moving forward

What surprised you most about your responses in the self-care worksheet?

_____

_____

_____

_____

_____

_____

_____

_____

Finally, write ONE action you will take THIS week to take more care of yourself

_____

_____

_____

_____

_____

_____

_____

_____

New Habit

Exercise and Yoga

We all know that physical fitness has a positive impact on mental health. However, it's difficult to stick to a fitness routine. What works for me is to do a 20 minute "bedside" routine as soon as I get up or before I get in the shower. Going to the gym just doesn't work for me. During this time, I clear my mind and think about all I am grateful for. I also do stretching and light exercises before bed. It's important for you to find what works for you and stick to it. Your life depends on it.

Meditation and/or prayer

One way I practice self-care is with the model called "ACTS". It is a thoughtful way to pray that helps you consistently give thanks before making requests of God. The acronym, that dates to at least 1883 (The Continent, 1883), stands for adoration, confess, thanksgiving, and supplication. I have added acknowledgement as the first step in praying.

ACTS PRAYER

Acknowledgement and adoration

Confess

Thanksgiving

Supplication

Accountability partner

Finally, it's important to have a mental health accountability partner in life. Someone who can remind you to slow down, smell the roses, and take it easy on yourself.

Reflection

Do you feel encouraged by your self-care plan and new habits? What else can you add to what you learned in this chapter? Who will be yourself care accountability partner?

_____

_____

_____

_____

_____

_____

_____

_____

Prosperity

8 Achieve Your Goals

Mantra

I am prosperous.

Challenge

If you could live your dream life, what would it look like? Sit there for a minute and enjoy the moment. Close your eyes and picture yourself there. Where are you? What do you see? Smell? Feel?

Quote

"Just because someone signed you up doesn't mean you have to do it. Learn to protect your time so that you can reach your goals." — Dr. Kisha Simmons

Objectives

1. How to focus on what's important

2. Create distraction-free work blocks

3. Daily and nightly must do's

What if you could learn new habits that stick and that help you accomplish your goals? Imagine how much happier you will feel if you could get more sleep at night and feel less rushed in the morning, all while achieving those goals that have been on the back burner. What would you do if you had more free time? It's time to live and be free! *Did you know that every 15 minutes of planning can yield an extra hour of time?*

People often ask me how I balance being a mom, professor, executive director of The Achiever Academy, speaker, consultant, activist and humanitarian. Well, I am still a work in progress, but several things help me. Some of these things may be new for you and others you are already accustomed to. The point is, spend time finding what works for you and stick to your plan.

Focusing on what's important.

I can't stress this enough... plan to spend time with those you love. Life is about experiences and I do this by planning travel. When I travel with friends and family I get a feeling of purpose and happiness that can't be replicated with other experiences. I have been lucky enough to have sailed on over 18 cruises and my sons have sailed on at least 5. My sons often say, "Mom, do you remember when we were on the Carnival Conquest and had the best cheese pizza?" Or, "I can't wait to see the baby Beluga again." Those memories are so vivid in their minds and we enjoy looking back at the photos and planning our next adventure at sea.

I'll never forget my first cruise. It was filled with excitement for being on a vessel so large and joy for the feeling of the warm sunshine on my face as I would sit on the deck and look out into the sea. One of the best experiences of my life was when I sailed the Mediterranean on a Norwegian ship. I was able to disconnect from back home (but enjoyed the fact that I could still call home to my children) and enjoy every moment of every day. When I returned from that experience, I vowed to find that same peace each day. Whether it's taking time to read on my kindle, cuddle up on the couch to a good movie, or take my boys around town to explore a new park or library, I have to stop working and start breathing.

How does the AchieveHer do it?

Calendar and email

I work in focused blocks. Outside of my teaching schedule, I dedicate time on my Google calendar to get stuff done. For me, research and service to the university are requirements. So, I block hours on specific days of the week to dedicate to those items. I schedule blocks of time for tasks.

Overhead tasks like email seem to sort themselves out but I must be deliberate about NOT checking it all throughout the day or else I get none of my major tasks accomplished. It's always a work in progress, but for me I know what works and what doesn't. I came up with a Rule of Email: RD3 which is only check email when you have time to Respond, Do, Delegate or Delete. Nothing causes me more stress than checking my email while in line at Kroger and realizing I have 10 emails to respond to. I wish I never opened my inbox! So, wait until you are at a point in which you can RD3! While we are at it:

Turn OFF email notifications

Turn OFF social notifications

Turn OFF app notifications

Stop being distracted by removing distractions. So what if someone just tagged you in a post. You don't have to be notified at that very moment. If you are going to be an AchieveHer and get stuff done, then you must have tunnel vision and focus.

When are you more focused and able to do deep work? Take a moment and write down when you work best (first thing in the morning, late at night). Then take time to job down work hours to work towards your goals.

_____

_____

_____

_____

_____

_____

_____

_____

Who are the most important people in your life and what are the most important things you must and would like to do with them?

_____

_____

_____

_____

_____

_____

_____

_____

What are the juiciest items on your Bucket List? (E.g. start a business? write a book?)

_____

_____

_____

_____

_____

_____

_____

List important projects/deadlines/deliverables over the next few months?

_____

_____

_____

_____

_____

_____

_____

_____

Now go to your electronic calendar or physical planner. Take time to schedule time to do the current quarter activities. You are simply NOT AVAILABLE – YOU ARE BOOKED!

Student Planner

I would be remiss if I didn't mention the best tool for those taking classes, the app I developed, Homework Suite student planner. Homework Suite was an easy to use academic planner that tracked classes, homework, and attendance. It had an import *syllabus* feature, social sharing, timetable and the ability to email teachers and study group members right from the app! Although this app is no longer available do to my many demands and other projects, I recommend that you search the app store for a similar solution.

Here are other organization tips for distraction-free work:

Mobile

Use a motivating screen saver

Go through your phone and delete unused apps (and turn off notifications)

Create folders and organize apps

Computer

Create effective file structures

Shortcuts to efficiency

Take 5 minutes to clean up your messy desktop

Move actual files to a folder (shortcut folder)

Back it up to the cloud or external hard rive

Protect your data with a secure password

New habits

On Sunday:

Write out your week at a glance on paper and keep it in your closet or on your vanity. This keeps you focused on what big meetings or projects you have coming due.

Set out and iron your clothes for the WEEK ahead. Use your week at a glance to plan your outfits. Don't forget underwear, sox, and belt!

Nightly

Before bed, think about your must-dos for tomorrow (write 5 pages in your book, write a blog post, work on your budget, etc.). These should be done at your productive time.

Write in your gratitude journal (refer to the gratitude journal).

Pray (refer to the acts prayer).

Reflection

What are your biggest time management hang-ups? What keeps you from working on your passion items or goals? Write them:

_____
_____
_____
_____
_____
_____
_____
_____

Now create an action for each hang-up. How will you combat procrastination and lack of motivation?

_____
_____
_____
_____
_____
_____

_____

_____

Go back through each chapter and secure your goals and new habits to your calendar. Which three goals or new habits are the most important to accomplish over the next three months? Write them below. Then, type them up and post them on your bathroom mirror, inside of your front door (so you see them on your way out) and as the screen saver on your phone.

_____

_____

_____

_____

_____

_____

_____

9 Education Changes Everything

Mantra

If I believed that I could, I would be _____.

Challenge

What's holding you back from being _____ (your answer from the mantra)? What did you do today to get you closer to being that person? What will you do tomorrow?

_____

_____

_____

_____

_____

_____

_____

_____

Objectives

1. Identify your biggest education challenges

2. Create a strategy to overcome your challenges

Quote

"Success isn't about how much money you make, it's about the difference you make in people's lives." — Michelle Obama

I t's Monday, Labor Day, and I just returned from a weekend trip to California to visit one of my sorority sisters and her mom. We laughed a lot, ate too much, and bonded over personal stories. One morning at breakfast, my friend's mother asked, "So why did you decide to become a professor?"

It's ironic because I never even wanted to attend college. I missed a lot of school because I was seriously unmotivated. I didn't live with either of my parents and living with different family members has a way of making you feel lonely and unstable. It made it difficult to have any hope for the future. I was sad and depressed and cried many nights. My grades were poor, along the lines of c's and d's and I routinely missed too many days of school to the point where I had to apply for a waiver to be promoted to a sophomore.

One day everything changed. One fall day in October 1995, I was walking the hall at school and a saw a flyer that read "Historically Black College Tour." I stepped closer and learned that during fall break, an organization was taking a small group of students on a weekend college tour. The tour was visiting Kentucky State University, Fisk University and Tennessee State University. I thought, "Hmmm, a bus trip sounds fun." The trip was highly subsidized, but I still needed to come up with a little money. So, I did some soliciting around my family and was able to gather up the money for the trip. That trip changed my life.

At the moment I stepped up on the tour bus and met our tour guide, my mindset changed. Something about the long bus ride made me start to imagine what kind of life I wanted for myself. And every time we touched down on a new campus, another spark was lit. I remember the student ambassadors sharing stories about the histories of the founding of the universities and what pride they had to be Black and how proud they were to be college-educated. I was overcome with pride, surprise and intrigue every time we visited a new campus.

I fell completely in love with Kentucky State University. The ironic thing is that I spent a few of my younger years living in Frankfort, KY with my mother and her second husband. The trip got better when we arrived in Nashville and visited Tennessee State University. I remember our student ambassador so clearly, explaining to us how much history has come from this very campus. From Wilma Rudolph to Oprah Winfrey, and so many legends between. She showed us dorm rooms, the cafeteria, and many buildings and classrooms on campus. And while each school was inspiring, there was something that just felt right about Tennessee State University. Our female student ambassador was wearing a blue sweater with the letters TSU and she was overjoyed to be able to share her experiences as a student with us as she toured us around campus. And I asked a question, "So you mean to tell me, we get a room, three meals a day, and I can study topics interesting to me?"

She replied with a smile, "Yes."

As we continued and walked the Floyd Payne Campus center, I noticed the blue and white signs and flyers, and students with backpacks and notebooks walking with purpose. For lunch, I fondly remember the cafeteria was serving us a soul food menu of greens, fried fish, and other home cooked delicacies. I thought to myself, I could see myself here as a college student. I'm just like the students here.

Something clicked. With every step, I knew Tennessee State was where I was supposed to be. I hadn't ever felt secure in my life until that moment. I knew I needed to take control of my future and live my life my way. I no longer cared about where my mother was or what she was doing. I didn't care why my father didn't work hard to spend time with me or the rest of the bickering or fighting in my family. All I wanted was to attend Tennessee State University (TSU)!

On the ride back to Indiana, I began believing in that dream to become a scholar because, if achieved, I knew I would always be able to care for myself and my needs. I went back to school laser-focused on getting to TSU. I went to class, asked questions, and worked hard to improve my grades. Spring rolled around, and the same organization did another college tour during the week of spring break. We visited Howard University, Morgan State University, Norfolk State University, Hampton University, Shaw University, St. Augustine University and North Carolina A&T University. Again, I was even more determined after returning from the trip. My junior year was filled with almost straight A's and a B here or there. That summer, I asked my aunt if we could take a road trip to for a final visit of the colleges I was considering. She said, "Baby girl, if you want to go to college, heck yeah, I'll drive you down there." So, she, my little cousin and I hit the road for TSU, Spelman and Clark Atlanta. My goal was to find out what it takes to be admitted and who I had to beg to pay for it! Once again, without a doubt, I fell more in love with TSU. It was something about that student center! It was so electric and exciting seeing educated blacks following behind some of the greatest people in history. And the rest is history. The day after my high school graduation, my mother and her husband at the time, drove me to Nashville and I started a summer precollege program. That fall I worked hard and achieved a 3.7 gpa my first semester as a computer science major. I had a lot of fun too, but there was no way I was going back home. My future was too bright to mess it up.

Some say, you don't need college to succeed. And yes, there are the stories of those who didn't finish college and became millionaires, but it is rare to be that successful without an education. I recommend going as far as you can with your education. More states are offering free or reduced tuition at community colleges.

Don't hesitate to take advantage of free training programs at accredited universities. There are also many credible online courses.

Who knew that one day I would be that unlikely face in front of the classroom lecturing, and that I would inspire and teach America's future business leaders. That dream has become a reality. And on a hot night in Oxford, Mississippi in May 2011, I felt larger than life, full of pride, walking across the stage at the University of Mississippi. On this campus I had faced overt racism and witnessed Ku Klux Klan rally's and nooses on trees. But none of that could stop me from getting an education.

After overcoming many obstacles during my childhood, battles with the graduate school admissions, getting married, financial strain, and having a son in my third year of my doctoral program, I became Dr. Lakisha Simmons!

I have known many people who have started college and stopped. If you are satisfied with your level of achievement in life and feel you have no further up to go, then great. But if you feel you could or should be making a lot more money, then you should finish your degree or go back for another degree. The sooner the better. If you are worried about loans, know that I took out loans every semester I attended college and I have paid off every cent. If it weren't for those loans I wouldn't have a degree and wouldn't make a quarter of what I make now. The return on that investment was more than worth it.

What is your biggest challenge with education?

_____

_____

_____

_____

_____

_____

_____

_____

List three strategies for eliminating that challenge.

_____

_____

_____

_____

_____

_____

_____

New Habit

Download a student planner app if you are enrolled in school. You won't regret it. Students have received positive student statistical results from the usage of reminder apps like Homework Suite. Research findings suggest that the perceived usefulness of Homework Suite Planner app positively predicted students' executive functioning, which is organization and time management skills. Increases in executive functioning due to the Homework Suite app led to more completed assignments, lower anxiety about forgetting homework assignments, and greater overall learning satisfaction with the course (*Lakisha Simmons, Amy Crook, Colin Cannonier & Chris Simmons (2018) There's an app for that: The impact of reminder apps on student learning and anxiety, Journal of Education for Business, 93:5, 185-195*).

Reflection

Do you have an unfinished educational dream? If so, what are you going to do about it? If not, what are you most grateful for doing education wise? Why?

_____

_____

_____

_____

_____

_____

_____

_____

10 Wealth Building

Mantra

I am disciplined with money.

Challenge

Reflection is an important and required skill for growth. Today and tomorrow, write down everything you spend (or have spent today). Carry around a sheet of paper and pen in your wallet so you can capture all purchases. Tomorrow review your purchases. What have you learned about your spending habits? Do you eat out a lot? Digital purchases? Shopping? Or necessities like gas for your car. Use this information to help you decide how you can be more efficient in your spending.

Spending Log

Date/Time	Item	Cost	Need or Want?

Quote

"You will have more money if you focus on experiencing life rather than spending your way through it." — Dr. Kisha Simmons

Objectives

1. Determine your financial goals

2. Check your credit report

3. Spend less money

4. Complete the 5-part plan to financial wealth

What are your financial goals? Do you have any? Now is the time to think about what you want out of life and create a financial plan to reach those goals. I am debt free and you can be too.

As a high school student, I knew that one day I would want to be financially stable, debt free, and travel the world. The most reasonable path in my mind at the time, was to have a lucrative career in the tech field. In college I majored in Computer Science. After changing majors a few times, I found my niche in the business school as an MIS major. Right out of college I obtained a job in a Fortune 100 company and was well on my way to a financially independent lifestyle. But what do you do when your income quickly increases? If you can't manage a little money you won't be able to manage a lot of money.

Name your three major financial goals:

_____

_____

_____

_____

_____

_____

_____

_____

Let's start by checking your credit report.

The Fair Credit Reporting Act (FCRA) requires each of the nationwide credit reporting companies — Equifax, Experian, and TransUnion — to provide you with a free copy of your credit report, at your request, once every 12 months. The FCRA promotes the accuracy and privacy of information in the files of the nation's credit reporting companies.

A credit report includes information on where you live, how you pay your bills, and whether you've been sued or have filed for bankruptcy. Nationwide credit reporting companies sell the information in your report to creditors, insurers, employers, and other businesses that use it to evaluate your applications for credit, insurance, employment, or renting a home.

The FCRA are providing free annual credit reports only through annualcreditreport.com. You must provide your name, address, social security number, and date of birth to verify your identity.

Your credit *score* is available for a fee. If you have a credit card, you can receive your credit score as a benefit of being a cardholder. Just call them and ask. Also, any time you apply for credit, the creditor must mail you a copy of your credit score. There is no need to purchase a credit score.

What did you learn by reviewing your report?

_____

_____

_____

_____

_____

_____

_____

_____

Here is my five-part plan to financial wealth:

1. Monthly Allowance

A real key to my financial success has been setting a limit on my discretionary income. I can spend every penny I have shopping online but that won't allow me to travel 5 or more times a year. I set a reasonable spending limit and put the cash in my wallet. Using cash helps me keep an eye on how much spending money I have left for the month.

I sometimes make online purchases because prices are cheaper and often there are no shipping charges. I allow myself a certain amount of allowance on my credit card that gets paid off every month. I do not carry a credit card balance month to month.

What's a reasonable amount of spending money for you per pay period? Why that amount?

_____

_____

_____

_____

_____

_____

_____

2. Liquid Savings Account

You need a liquid cash savings that you can easily access when needed, and this savings account should never fall below at least 6 months of expenses. If you could create no income for six months, you could still maintain your standard of living and not get behind on your bills. While you are building this, pay at least the minimum due on your debt bills.

As a college student you may not have much income and thus not much to save. But it's important to create the habit so you must save something each time you get paid or get a windfall. You must have some money to fall back on.

If you are sustaining a household, calculate your monthly expenses including groceries, gas, household necessities and monthly allowance. This is your Liquid Savings Account goal. Aim to save this amount in the next 12 months.

Monthly Expenses x 6 months = _____ / 12 = $ to save each month (after taxes)

3. Retirement Investing

Immediately, as in my first paycheck, I invested in my company's 401k plan. A 401k plan (depending on industry may be called something else, e.g. 403b) is a *retirement savings account that grows from uninsured investments*. And the money is invested in stocks, bonds, or mutual funds which have no guarantee for returns and there will be ups and downs in the market, but over the length of a career most people average an 8% return on their investments.

Growth Example:

CNN Money has a great example: Suppose you set aside $1,000 a year (about $19 a week) when you're 25. You put it in a retirement account earning 7% a year. Even if you stop investing completely when you turn 35 - that is, you've invested for only 10 years - your total investment will have grown to nearly $113,000 by the time you turn 65 and are ready to retire. That's right: A $10,000 investment turns into $113,000.

Let's say you do the same exact thing, but you don't start investing the $1,000 a year until you turn 35. And you keep on investing that much every single year until you turn 65. You invest $1,000 a year for 30 years, rather than for 10 years as in the previous example. How much do you wind up with when you're 65? Only about $101,000. That's right, even though you invest three times as much money, you wind up with less.

The earlier you start investing, the more you can benefit from compounding. That's why you need to get going as soon as possible. You can't touch it until retirement age (without a penalty). But that's okay because you also will save money in a personal savings account.

Retirement Investing. Discover if your company offers a retirement plan such as a pension or 401k plan. If they do, ask if they match your contribution. Most companies offer retirement plans and match. Contribute at least 10% of your income (pretax) into that company-sponsored plan. This is how you save for the long-term. Entrepreneurs should contribute to a tax-deferred plan on their own.

4. Debt reduction plan

Your goal is to have positive net worth, so you can live a life of prosperity and freedom. We cannot do that with unsecured debt (credit cards, small loans) keeping us up at night. The first course of action is to take an inventory of all your debt and put a halt on unnecessary debt. Unnecessary debt are things that you want but not that you need to reach your goals in life. In my personal opinion, student loans to pay tuition and living expenses are necessary. Without student loans, I would have never received my bachelor's or Ph.D. Degree.

If you use a credit card, make sure you have only one credit card and check the balance every Monday. This helps you realize just how much and how fast debt can accumulate. And choose your card wisely. Since I travel a great deal. It only makes sense I choose a card that gives me airline points for each dollar spent.

Always pay your bills and debts on time, even if it's just the minimum due. Never skip a month or pay late. Those bad habits ruin your credit score.

From your credit report, list all your debts and the total amounts due on a sheet of paper (order by smallest to largest debt owed).

Debt   **Amount**

_____

_____

_____

_____

_____

Total _____

5. Other Income & Investments

An AchieveHER always has multiple streams of income! Think about the ways you can make your money work for you. Especially if you are a college AchieveHER, think about a side hustle that plays on your talents and fits into your schedule. Can you give great manicures or pedicures? College AchieveHers love to carry themselves as elegant ladies and a mani pedi is usually a top priority. Are you an excellent proofreader? I bet you can offer an editing service and could gain at least one client from every class you are in. Are you strong in math? Many students need a math tutor. Think smart, not hard! And find ways to make additional cash to sustain yourself through college.

Once you graduate, keep the hustle going. After all the above is accounted for, begin investing in other vehicles such as the stock market, real estate, a business, or in someone's start up. Remember, an AchieveHer always has multiple streams of income! Start a brokerage account with low cost index funds at Vanguard or Fidelity and let it grow over the years. Compound interest is your friend.

I also recommend doing something related to your passions. That way you feel fulfilled as well as accumulate additional cash to pay down debt or accumulate wealth. At this stage in your life your time is worth a lot so think of a digital business or more passive income streams.

List three side hustle ideas:

Now let's work on a budget. This budget is simple and straightforward and broken down into sections.

The first section, Prior Balances, is a space for you to track prior month balances and add what you are able to save this month (or your specific pay period). Income is where you will add all of your sources of income for the pay period. Third, list all of your expenses. Don't leave out anything. Fourth, account for your savings and investment goals. Lastly, there is a section to budget for specific items, perhaps a new laptop, trip, or automobile.

January Year			Deposit	New Totals
Prior Balances				
	Liquid Savings	$ 1,000.00	$ 250.00	$ 1,250.00
	Checking			$ -
				$ -
				$ -
	Total	$1,000.00	$250.00	$1,250.00
Income				
	Job			$4,000.00
	Side Hustle			$500.00
			Total	$4,500.00
Expenses				
Paid	**Transaction**		**Amount**	**Balance**
	Rent			$4,500.00
	Insurance			$4,500.00
	Grocery			$4,500.00
	Power			$4,500.00
	Student Loans			$4,500.00
	Auto Loan			$4,500.00
	Mobile Phone			$4,500.00
	Spotify			$4,500.00
	Dropbox			$4,500.00
				$4,500.00
				$4,500.00
				$4,500.00
				$4,500.00
				$4,500.00
				$4,500.00
				$4,500.00
		Total	$0.00	$4,500.00
Savings & Investments				**Balance**
	Liquid Savings			$4,500.00
	Business			$4,500.00
				$4,500.00
				$4,500.00
				$4,500.00
		Total	$0.00	$4,500.00
Budget for Items				**Balance**
	Down payment for car			$4,500.00
				$4,500.00
				$4,500.00
				$4,500.00
		Total	$0.00	$4,500.00

You can download an electronic copy from Dr. Kisha's website (www.lakishasimmons.com/the-unlikely-achieveher). After you've finalized the spreadsheet, copy the sheet and rename it as the next month.

New Habit

Use the Budget worksheet! Review this worksheet every two weeks to ensure you are staying on track. Is it helping you? If so, I'd love to hear how. Email me or tell your story on social media and tag me. Good luck.

Reflection

How do you feel about your current financial situation?

_____
_____
_____
_____
_____
_____
_____
_____

What are your short and long term goals?

_____
_____
_____
_____
_____
_____

Do you have a strategy to meet your short and long-term financial goals?

Use the space below to map out your plans.

_____

_____

_____

_____

_____

_____

_____

_____

_____

Lakisha L. Simmons, Ph.D.

11 Achieve A Successful Career

Mantra

My work and my life are important. I was here.

Challenge

What is my dream work? Why am I drawn to that work?

_____

_____

_____

_____

_____

_____

_____

_____

Quote

And he said, the things which are impossible with men are possible with God.
— Luke 18:27 KJV

Objectives

1. Be poised and positioned to win

2. Dress as a part of your strategy

3. Persistently overcome obstacles

4. Negotiate into prosperity

W
hat are you doing with your life? What are you going to do next with your life? This chapter is all about getting to your dream career. It takes sometimes a few different careers before you find what that is. You may get a degree in a field and start working in it and realize it was a mistake (can anyone relate?). Other times, you find that the work you started with was a necessary building block on the path to your ultimate destination.

When maneuvering through life to achieve your dream lifestyle, you must be poised and persistent. If you stay the course and persevere, you will reach prosperity. Let me give you some tips in each area.

Be poised and positioned to win

When starting your own business or interviewing for a job, you must have mastered the tools in section one of this book. But there are some specific job-related esteem building tools you can use to walk into the interview prepared to sell yourself. Many people have heard of a SWOT analysis by Albert Humphrey which allows a company to assess its strengths, weaknesses, opportunities, and threats. Here, we can use this same thought process to assess our competitive ability and plan according. Complete the following personal SWOT analysis.

My Personal SWOT Analysis			
		Characteristics	
		Favorable	Unfavorable
SWOT	Internal: Within my control.	My Strengths:	My Weaknesses:
	External: In the marketplace.	Opportunities for me:	Threats working against me:
Goals	My career goals	Personal Goals:	
	My desired position	Job Description:	
	My competitive Advantages	What sets me apart from other job applicants:	

Dress as a part of your strategy

Be aware of what message you are sending with your dress. Personal branding is intentional whether on purpose or by accident. Find out what is acceptable in your career of choice. Do the research to see what successful people in the field wear. I am not saying change who you are, but appropriate clothing will make a difference in how you are perceived. For example, if you are going into a formal business meeting, wear something that represents business, like a suit, work dress, etc. Depending on the company, you may need to stay more conservative to not distract from the words you are saying. For typical conservative business meetings, I wear black, blue, brown and grey as my suit color (as mentioned in the body language chapter). I may add a pop of color to show my personality depending on the event. A hot pink blouse may be too distracting at a business meeting or a construction company meeting, but may be more appropriate at a women's empowerment meeting. Just know the audience and the message you want to send. It's about strategy on your end to be not only seen but also heard. Is it fair to have to do all this? No, but as women, we must strategize to get where we want to be.

Persistently overcome obstacles

Let's say you've landed your dream job. Now what? You will soon run up against your first set of challenges either with process and red tape, learning institutional knowledge, or butting heads with people. Your first step should be to understand the culture of the organization. Culture is everything because it gives you insight into what makes or breaks that company and who goes to the top. Culture is like the fabric that binds a family. It's the behaviors and values that represent that company. Corporate etiquette varies by company. When you understand the culture, you can apply the correct corporate etiquette. For example, in some organizations I worked in, it was corporate etiquette to talk to someone in person before sending them a written request to do something. Otherwise, don't expect a response. This brings me to my next must-do item to succeed in your career and for a successful life, seek mentors.

Find two mentors

In every pursuit, I've sought a professional mentor before jumping in. Find someone in the position you want to be in and then make it easy for them to mentor you. Before becoming a Six Sigma Black Belt, I closely studied and befriended a young woman on a path I wanted to follow. I built a rapport with her, contacted her often, we went to lunch every now and again. She was always open to sharing how she handled her challenges and successes and I appreciated her for that. She was a great professional mentor.

Find a personal life mentor. Who is a woman who may not be in your field, but is just a great role model for you? Maybe she is great at juggling a lot and shows style and grace while doing it. Maybe she has great relationship advice and you admire her class. You'd be surprised by how many women would love to mentor you. No matter how old we get, there is someone out there who's been where we are and can help us get where we want to go.

Be prosperous

How to negotiate job offers

Many women are afraid to ask for more money than is offered. This is a well-known fact that men negotiate better than women. In a study by Glassdoor, 68% of women accepted the first salary they were offered versus 52% of men (Glassdoor.com). Men are asking for more, and while not every job will give more, you certainly won't get more if you don't ask. This is where knowing your value comes in (refer to your prior SWOT analysis).

You also must know what the average starting salary is for that position. Do your research online and even call headhunters or contact people on LinkedIn. How will you know if you are being lowballed? If you know the average salary, you can more effectively negotiate because you can say, "With my education and credentials I believe I am more in line with xyz salary," and thus counter offer.

Don't obsess over the salary and forget about other perks. Know your must-haves in life, such as more vacation days so you can travel or tuition reimbursement so that you can receive an advanced education. When I was offered a job at a new institution, I asked for a specific amount higher and received a little less than what I asked but was still more than the offer. I also asked to count teaching time at a previous university as time credit with my new university and that negotiation was accepted. You never know unless you ask. And if you are afraid that if you ask for a reasonable salary or accommodation that the company will retract the offer, that is not a place you want to work anyway.

Rewrite your mission statement from the Passion and Purpose chapter. Do you need to add anything?

_____

_____

_____

_____

_____

_____

_____

_____

New Habit

Decide who you want to be, what you want to be known for, and live authentically. Don't work somewhere you can't be yourself (if you do, make sure it is a short-term strategy). Speak to the universe and position yourself around people, who can help you reach your goals. On social media, follow and set it up where you see content first from those that can help you reach your pinnacle.

Reflection

Are you living your dream life? Why or why not?

_____

_____

_____

_____

_____

_____

_____

_____

Final Words Of Encouragement

In all of your days, what is the one moment in which you felt most achieved? Just when I feel I've accomplished everything possible; I surprise myself. From birthing two baby boys to obtaining a Ph.D., founding an app business (Homework Suite) and a nonprofit (The Achiever Academy), being awarded tenure as a professor, and a sought-after leadership trainer and speaker I never knew I could feel any more accomplished. On Thursday, March 8, 2018, which was International Women's Day, The Achiever Academy (TAA) hosted a special assembly for over 200 female students at a local high school in Nashville, TN. This event, specifically scheduled to coincide with International Women's Day, was developed as an inaugural community service experience for TAA participants. TAA cultivates college and career achieveHers to give back to girls in local communities by donating their time and resources. But we had no idea of the impact we would make.

The assembly consisted of a workshop I titled "My Possible Goals" and was meant to teach the girls how to set and achieve goals. It is a workshop I created for women that I tailored to high school girls. It was also meant to inspire and motivate them to dream beyond what they think is possible. Many girls who are in economically disadvantaged areas tend to dream to be only what their close friends and family have become. Students also downloaded a homework planner app to help them get organized and track their homework. Finally, I talked to them about what it means to be a woman and we brainstormed all the ways in which we are phenomenal. As a way to drive that point home and eliminate the stigma around periods, I concluded the event by giving away packages of period products to each of the girls (over 200). I had been charging "5 packages of period products" as the ticket price for my TAA events and workshops for several months in preparation for a big donation to the girls. Many friends, family and even strangers across social media donated products and cash towards the purchase of the additional period products that I needed. After the event, we asked some of the girls what they took away from the event. One senior responded that no one had ever talked to her about goals before. I knew at that moment, I had finally achieved.

Life is not only about achieving personal accolades, but more so about what you do to elevate someone else's life. What are you doing to help others reach their highest level? My family practitioner once told me that he was proud of me for starting a nonprofit so young in life. He said to me "now you will start to realize your fullest potential because your focus is on others". I believe that to be true.

It's personal mission to equip and empower girls and women to reach their full potential. That's why I started The Achiever Academy and my training company BRAVE Consulting, to develop poised, persistent and prosperous women.

Soon after the International Women's day event, I learned that 43% of the students in the Metropolitan Nashville Public Schools (MNPS) were economically disadvantaged (on government assistance) and of those are 67% are black or Hispanic. I felt that I had to do something with a bigger impact, but what? Nearly five months later *The Tennessean* newspaper reported on the number of girls missing school due to lack of affordable access to period protection products. I was featured in the article due to my period projects and work around the issue. With the attention of the article, came many concerned citizens who wanted a way to get involved. I decided to launch the Nashville Period Project, a month-long, city-wide awareness and donation effort.

The Nashville Period Project had two goals. First, to raise awareness around period poverty and reduce the stigma around menstruation. The second, was to collect and stock a large supply of period protection products for girls who attend Metro Nashville Public Schools. On the last Saturday of September 2018, we held the donation drop off event at the MNPS warehouse. Over 35 teams from local organizations had signed up to bring donations and after almost all of it was counted, we had collected over 200,000 period products! The products were to be distributed to the 11 middle and high schools on the MNPS priority list. These are the 'at risk" schools that receive Title I funding and are among the bottom 5% in academic achievement. While 200,000 products may seem like a lot, it is a drop in the bucket considering this will serve the 2,900 students for only 2-3 monthly cycles. There is more work to be done to improve the quality of life and to equal the education playing field.

I consider the lack of access to period products an access to education issue. Our girls can't develop into prosperous women if they are missing school. When school-age girls get their period, they sometimes miss school if they don't have the period products that they need, and there is nowhere to get free period products. A study by Always has shown that 1 in 5 girls has missed school due to a lack of access to period products. Even if a girl can afford them, but gets her period unexpectedly, she will have to leave class and potentially miss the rest of the school day. That is a day she is now behind her peers.

I have started the Green Period to educate girls and women about reusable and sustainable period products. I recommend five types of reusable menstrual products that are better for your body, better for your purse and better for the environment. Learn more in my Green Period class at www.LakishaSimmons.com. View my recommended reusable menstrual products online at http://amazon.com/shop/drkishasimmons.

I say all of this to express to you that there are so many issues around us and that we can make a difference. To reach your fullest potential and happiness, focus on helping others. Life is bigger than oneself. To love others, you must first love yourself. I leave you with this last activity, a time for self-love. Make copies and complete it every so often to remind you that no matter from where you came, or what experiences you've had, you are worthy to be loved and capable of changing the world, as an AchieveHer.

Sincerely,

Dr. Kisha

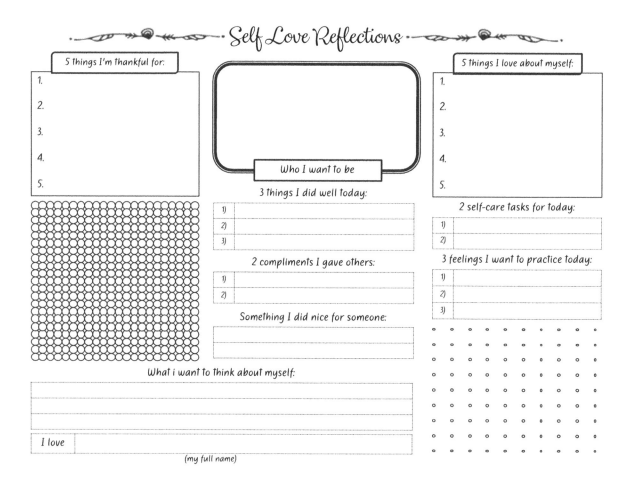

About The Author

D r. Lakisha L. Simmons is an expert in business intelligence and analytics. She is the CEO of BRAVE Consulting training company, founder of Homework Suite App for students, 6 Sigma Black Belt (Caterpillar, Inc), and associate professor of management information systems at Belmont University with over 40 peer-reviewed scholarly works. Dr. Kisha's platform centers on keeping girls in school and successful and developing women personally and professionally. Dr. Simmons spends a great deal of her time mentoring, training and speaking to women about personal and professional development. She is an active member of Delta Sigma Theta Sorority, Inc., Faculty Member of The PhD Project, and Beta Gamma Sigma International.

Dr. Kisha has won numerous research, teaching and service awards including the 2019 Nashville Business Journal 40 Under 40 Award, 2019 Tennessee State University Young Alumni Award 40 Under 40, 2018 Nashville Emerging Leader in Education Award by the Nashville Chamber of Commerce, 2018 Rising Star Award by the Nashville Black Chamber of Commerce, and 2018 Susan Short Jones Emerging Leaders Award by the National Coalition of 100 Black Women, Inc Metro Nashville Chapter. Contact Dr. Kisha at www.LakishaSimmons.com and on social media @drkishasimmons.

Made in the USA
Las Vegas, NV
04 April 2021